String Quarte.

in D minor

Op.42

By

Joseph Haydn

A Score for Strings

1785

British Library Cataloguing-in-Publication Data
A catalogue record for this book is available from
the British Library

Op. 42, in D Minor

I

II

Trio

Menuetto D. C.

III

Adagio e cantabile

IV

Finale
Presto